POETRY Wonderland

Voices From Kent

Edited By Brixie Payne

First published in Great Britain in 2019 by:

Young Writers® Est. 1991

Young Writers
Remus House
Coltsfoot Drive
Peterborough
PE2 9BF
Telephone: 01733 890066
Website: www.youngwriters.co.uk

All Rights Reserved
Book Design by Spencer Hart
© Copyright Contributors 2019
SB ISBN 978-1-78988-551-4
Printed and bound in the UK by BookPrintingUK
Website: www.bookprintinguk.com
YB0406E

FOREWORD

Here at Young Writers, we love to let imaginations run wild and creativity go crazy. Our aim is to encourage young people to get their creative juices flowing and put pen to paper. Each competition is tailored to the relevant age group, hopefully giving each pupil the inspiration and incentive to create their own piece of creative writing, whether it's a poem or a short story. By allowing them to see their own work in print, we know their confidence and love for the written word will grow.

For our latest competition Poetry Wonderland, we invited primary school pupils to create wild and wonderful poems on any topic they liked – the only limits were the limits of their imagination! Using poetry as their magic wand, these young poets have conjured up worlds, creatures and situations that will amaze and astound or scare and startle! Using a variety of poetic forms of their own choosing, they have allowed us to get a glimpse into their vivid imaginations. We hope you enjoy wandering through the wonders of this book as much as we have.

CONTENTS

Holy Trinity Lamorbey CE Primary School, Sidcup

Matthew Robinson (7)	1
Holly Watson (10)	2
Olivia Gray (10)	4
Osinachi Edovia (7)	6
Lucy Bunting (11)	8
Matthew George Heyburn (11)	10
Dylan Iley (9)	12
Ellie Wong (8)	14
Aubrey Oliver Blegvad Ward (7)	16
Marcus Hoang (7)	17
Ishita Chhabra (10)	18
Kane Wakeling (7)	20
Olivia Ferdinand-Brown (8)	21
Oliver Samuel Drury (9)	22
Freddie Bell (10)	24
Harry Benson (11)	25
Jethro Nanjo (7)	26
Kate Smith (11)	27
Avaani Dutta (9)	28
Thomas Harding (8)	30
Hetty Harrison (9)	31
Ellie Shaw (8)	32
Archie Lee Downton (9)	33
Sam Jackson (9)	34
Ava Spooner (8)	36
Albert Charles Paskins (9)	37
Josephus Nanjo (9)	38
Lewis James Farrow (11)	40
Sam Morgan (7)	41
Isatu Barrie (10)	42
Benedict Keeley (10)	43
Freddie Grange (9)	44
Teddy Brient (8)	45
Jada Annan (11)	46
Grace Stewart (10)	47
Lisa Nyandusi (9)	48
Valentina Hin (8)	49
Holly Lucy Evens (9)	50
George Panter (9)	51
Damilare Oshin (10)	52
Sinclair Dikeocha (11)	53
Magda Augustowska (11)	54
Sophie Scanlon (11)	56
Percy Cavanagh (9)	57
Fola Edgal (8)	58
Daisy Meir (10)	59
Emily Frowde (10)	60
Isobella Dixon (11)	61
Lucy Sullivan (11)	62
Elliot Martin (11)	63
Macie Alana Davey (11)	64
Eva Wells (9)	65
Ava Green (8)	66
Holly Highmore (9)	67
Chloe Louise Wing Yan Tse (10)	68
Munachiso Onyeanusi (8)	69
Theodore Andreas Georgiou (10)	70
Harry Beerling (9)	71
Grace Foden (11)	72
Dami Olofinlua (8)	73
Grace Elouise Shaw (8)	74
Eimear O'Mahony (8)	75
Blake McIntosh (7)	76
Luke Hutchins (8)	77
Eleanor-Rose Delaney (9)	78
Abdulmuqeet Sulaimon (8)	79
Joshua Walters (9)	80
Isabelle Harding (9)	81

Albie King (8)	82
Ivy Lee (9)	83
Harry George (9)	84
Joel Unger (9)	85
Charlie Workman (9)	86
Abdulmateen Sulaimon (10)	87
Shaun Miles (11)	88
Emma Anthony (8)	89
Poppy Back (7)	90
James Dixon (9)	91
Zara Eleanor Lin Heyburn (8)	92
Katherine Childs (10)	93
Amaya Vongswang (9)	94
Semilore Akinfe (8)	95
Aoife Reilly (11)	96
Daisy Macangus (8)	97
Chloe Ella Parr (10)	98
Georgie Stanley McMahon (10)	99
Lucas Kai Davids-Ruiz (8)	100
Pagan Honeywell (9)	101
Stanley Swan (8)	102
Jermaine Annan (8)	103
Freddie Palmer (9)	104

Jubilee Primary School, Maidstone

Reuben Yves-Louis Mundell (9)	105
Thomas Hugo-Ross Mundell (8)	106
Nathan Molloy (9)	107
Poppy Schofield (9)	108
Leon Elijah Price (9)	109
Eden Longley (9)	110
Ciara Katrina Denise Jane Crittall (9)	111
Harrison Jones (8)	112
Ross Benjamin Price (8)	113
Maya Fawzy (9)	114
Neave Elliott (8)	115
Pearl Deri Hepworth (8)	116
Eulalie Sylvie Mundell (8)	117
Aryan Ahmed (8)	118
Haven Thandiwe Fesshaie (8)	119
Matthew James Rich (9)	120

St Peter-In-Thanet CE Junior School, St Peters

Oliver Milchard (7)	121
Daisy May Websper (7)	122
Frankie Staveley (10)	124
Lilia Mai Harris (10)	126
Hettie Mabel Hunt (10)	128
Maisie Biggs (7)	130
Lily Skinner (10)	132
Calliope Hamilton (9)	134
George Randall (11)	135
Macy Ann Martin (9)	136
Michaela Murphy (11)	137
Layla Bartlett (10)	138
Thomas Pike (10)	140
Marlie-Anne McGregor (9)	141
Riley Evans (9)	142
Luke Hopson (9)	143
Teaghan Dooley (11)	144
Katherine Jenkins (10)	145
Aurora Short (7)	146
Oliver Setterfield (10)	147
Mercie Miller (9)	148
Ethan Nicholas Cobley (9)	149
James Dowdeswell (10)	150
Evie Van Jensen (9)	151
Bradley Tournay (10)	152
Thomas Girdler (9)	153
Harlan Groombridge (9)	154
Niamh Lily Carroll (9)	155
Rex Beevers (9)	156
Sophia Poppy Davidge (8)	157
Sam Gibson (9)	158
Mason Buckingham (10)	159
Mia-Brooke Aimee Page (8)	160

Temple Mill Primary School, Strood

Faida Aghogho Okotete (11)	161
Rebecca Bragg (11)	162
Henry Williams (10)	164
Martin Poprelkov (11)	165

The Granville School, Sevenoaks

Chloe Tippin (8)	166
Harriet Mackenzie (8)	168
Lexie Beck (8)	169
Madeleine Soong (7)	170
Isabel Mclain (7)	171
Jessica Dowell (7)	172
Amelie Cassidy (7)	173
Alexandra Rose Sinclair (7)	174

Upton Primary School, Bexley

Maya Jheeta (7)	175
Maya Fahim (10)	176
Gunjan Uppal (8)	179
Masha Strazdina (9)	180
Arisha Rahman (9)	182
Liana Wallace (8) & Esmee Jones (9)	184

The Poems

Pompeii

I wake up and it is no ordinary day
so I take my time machine
and head to Pompeii.

Then Pompeii blows up
my hotel explodes
I start running away
while the path erodes!

I'm nearly three-quarters dead
I'm still able to move
so I pick up my time machine
I get kicked by a hoof.

Then an army comes marching
the troops, the team, the squad
nearly kills me
but I take up my time machine.

So now I know from my visit to Pompeii
that I will never come
to this landmark again!

Matthew Robinson (7)
Holy Trinity Lamorbey CE Primary School, Sidcup

What You Can See In Space

Mercury is the closest to the sun,
That does not mean it is as hot as a bun.

If you zoom out into space,
It is like an endless race.

Venus spins the opposite way,
And has the brightest days.

If you zoom out into space,
It is like an endless race.

Earth is so very different,
It is a square that's bent.

If you zoom out into space,
It is like an endless race.

It is so very hot on Mars,
It is like sitting on stars.

If you zoom out into space,
It is like an endless race.

Jupiter is so big,
It is bigger than a pig.

If you zoom out into space,
It is like an endless race.

Saturn has so many rings,
Some of them might even go *ding!*

If you zoom out into space,
It is like an endless race.

Uranus is up the air,
So when you go, take care.

If you zoom out into space,
It is like an endless race.

Neptune is a fun trip
Just be careful you don't get a nip.

If you zoom out into space,
It is like an endless race.

Holly Watson (10)
Holy Trinity Lamorbey CE Primary School, Sidcup

A Trip To Space!

The darkness surrounded me
as I left Earth's atmosphere,
I started to feel dizzy as we started to lose gravity,
We opened the doors to the rocket,
But there and then, the other astronaut's eyes
nearly fell out of their sockets!

We turned around to see a rocky path of wonder
and amazement... it was the moon!
The moon is a moon, an icon on its own,
It doesn't need a planet
or a star to look good from afar.

Our very own moon, it controls the waves,
hides in our days,
It brightens up the night
but doesn't make its own light,
I realised the moon is a sunflower
in a crop of daisies,
As it stands out in the field of stars.

Catching a suntan by the surface of the sun
was good and all,

But I think it was more of a sunburn!
I found a tiny room in our rocket to keep me safe
while we were out in this dangerous place,
And this is what I did... I had a sleep in space!

I brushed my teeth and ate space beef,
I travelled deeper into the Milky Way,
And the first thing I did was take a big bite *mmm!*
The Milky Way tasted amazing!
I got back in my rocket
and the worst thing happened...

I started to hurtle towards the sun!
Then my life flashed before my eyes and I
realised... I was way too lazy!
To make matters worse, a satellite came crashing
through the sky and it nearly made me die,
I thought it was the end
till an alien came to save me,
But it turns out, he just wanted to eat me...

Olivia Gray (10)
Holy Trinity Lamorbey CE Primary School, Sidcup

Numberblocks

Numberblocks, Numberblocks, here I come,
Add yourselves together, I mean do the sum,
Let's play with one,
Let's be the sun,
Let's dance with two,
Let's wear a shoe,
Let's tango with three,
Let's dance with a bee,
Let's play peekaboo with four,
Let's open the door,
Let's sing with five,
Let's go to the beehive,
Let's part with six,
Let's joint the mix,
Let's march with seven,
Let's go to Heaven,
Let's save the day with eight,
But oh no, we're late!
Let's follow nine
Let's climb a vine,

Let's count to ten,
Let's visit a hen.

Osinachi Edovia (7)
Holy Trinity Lamorbey CE Primary School, Sidcup

The Land Of Far Beyond

Beneath your feet sleeps a mystical land
which Sinbad discovered,
This bewitching place is a dream-like world
waiting to be uncovered,
A colourless, pure, glassy lagoon
sprinkled with sausage-shaped fish,
A showering cloudless waterfall spilling into it,
Six miniature doughnut-like stepping stones
guiding Sinbad across,
Towering candy cane-trunked trees
burdened with chocolate gold,
Positively trembling with excitement,
he scampered over, bold,
Suddenly, an unreal creature
guarding its beloved treasure,
Charged at Sinbad with its dragon head,
way too tall to measure,
Shaking with fear, Sinbad disposed of his riches
and sprinted for dear life,
He reached in his belt in complete distress,
searching for a knife,

But before he could do so,
it started to rain, rain like mad!
The giant drops that came shooting down
were gumballs and hurt bad,
Luckily for Sinbad, he managed to escape,
though he never got the treasure,
But hopefully this experience
has taught him a lesson forever and ever!

Lucy Bunting (11)
Holy Trinity Lamorbey CE Primary School, Sidcup

The Invincible Sailor

Of all the places Sinbad had been,
This was the best of all he had seen...
When he'd first decided to buy a ship,
He thought it was nice to make a friendship.

The ship he bought,
Soon was caught,
The birds flying high in the sky,
Were being ever so sly.

All the rocks flying by,
Were all falling out of the sky,
It was unusual for Sinbad to see,
That rocks were walking, people fled.

When the rocks had stopped falling,
The wreckage was appalling,
When Sinbad saw the wood,
He never really understood.

When the fish rushed past him,
They made him want to swim,

The sun started to slaughter him,
And he could resist a swim.

Sinbad floated on a log,
Soon passing a sticky bog,
As he approached some land,
It reminded him of a beach of sand.

When he got up and smelt the air,
He climbed a tree and found a pear,
He made a fire to keep him warm,
Then he decided to pray on the cut lawn.

Matthew George Heyburn (11)
Holy Trinity Lamorbey CE Primary School, Sidcup

Space Race

Fishing off a planet, catching nothing but moons,
Frying cheesy moon rocks, *mmm* yummy!
Learning to speak alien, a wonderful tongue,
Blowing bubbles into moon rocks,
hoping aliens are okay with it,
The moon is a giant's bogey, *ew!*
Mars is looking like a cookie
and Uranus is a burger,
When you dream in space, you watch a race,
Skipping on a rocket,
getting sick between asteroids,
Skiing on Saturn's rings so fast,
getting torn limb from limb,
Getting a tan on the sun, more like sunburn!
Scuba-diving in the moon's craters
and meeting aliens,
An alien BBQ in space, a terrific feast!
Pandas in space, what a terrific race,
Aliens, what great personalities,
Drinking from the Milky Way,
getting fitter by the second,

Getting smashed by Titan with his boomerang,
Neptune is a blue cookie getting chased by Earth,
Neptune is a bear chasing the Goldilocks planet,
Flying past like a shooting star.

Dylan Iley (9)
Holy Trinity Lamorbey CE Primary School, Sidcup

The Rainforest Animals

If I were a monkey,
I could see the blue sky above the trees.
If I were a sloth, all I could see would be the food in
front of me and the high trees towering higher
than the top of my head.
If I were a fish, I could see
the deep underwater sea.
If I were a spider, I could see
the flies flying into my trap, he, he, he!
If I were a jaguar, I could see
the others ahead of me.
If I were a poison dart frog,
I could hear parrots screeching
to warn their friends about me.
If I were a macaw, I could hear my mates
playing very friendly.
If I were a happy eagle, I could hear
everyone arguing, what a screech!
If I were an alligator,
I could hear people screaming at me.
If I were a snake, I could smell the fresh air.

If I were a tarantula, I could smell my sticky web.
If I were a panther, I could feel the wind
against my back.
If I were a bug, I could feel the soil
softly pressing on my feet.

Ellie Wong (8)
Holy Trinity Lamorbey CE Primary School, Sidcup

Meeting Footballers

I want to meet a footballer tall and strong
Today is the day my footballers are coming
I hear a sound, *ding-dong!*
I'm going to Paris, hooray!

I'm in the Paris stadium
It looks epic
I want to play here
I don't have a ball.

Neymar, Mbappé, they're not here
When are they coming?
Oh, they're here!

"Have you got my signed shirt?"
"Yes, here it is," says Mbappé
"Have you got my picture?"
"Yes, I have it," says Neymar.

Aubrey Oliver Blegvad Ward (7)
Holy Trinity Lamorbey CE Primary School, Sidcup

Build Your Lego But Become Your Lego

I was building Lego when,
in a second of yellow, I became it!
I ran wild, desperately shouting, "Where am I?"
but, in a second, a rock became a house!
The mountain became an enormous city centre!
The grass became a city station in one second,
What a rare treat for me,
Just the right time for me,
What a cool treat,
With me standing in the street,
It was time to go forwards,
time to go to the future,
I whizzed through time till I went forwards,
I came in the elevator time machine,
then built everything,
From train stations to city centres
with just my hands.

Marcus Hoang (7)
Holy Trinity Lamorbey CE Primary School, Sidcup

The Secrets Of Space

In the deep velvet of space, comets are flung,
Aliens converse in a different tongue,
The stars are little fireflies, illuminating the sky,
Through millions of galaxies, shooting stars fly.

The sun shines its bright face,
Disappearing in the evening with no trace,
The sun beams down on us, ready to set soon,
It travels down like a hot air balloon.

Mighty meteors hurtle down with a bang,
Like on a washing line, planets hang,
Saturn has a prominent ring to behold,
Neptune washes us with oceans so cold.

The moon is an owl's eye, staring at the Earth,
Millions of pounds, planets are worth,
People float about carelessly,
Taking advantage of no gravity.

The darkness is eerie, it encloses the rockets,
Astronauts' eyes popping out of their sockets,

NASA prepares for yet another mission,
Astronauts getting ready for their expedition!

Ishita Chhabra (10)
Holy Trinity Lamorbey CE Primary School, Sidcup

Jumanji

Fall through a jungle hole into Jumanji,
And get the protection
and go to a level with your friend,
And go and explore and fly high in the sky,
If you complete all the levels,
you'll win one billion pounds,
If you complete all the levels, jump high in the sky,
And fall into the sea with a big splash,
See a dog hug a frog,
Drive a Ferrari really fast,
You should fight a monster and fantastically win,
And be a billionaire and fly in a helicopter,
Jet ski and jump from so high up,
And fall with a parachute,
Make a tree house and sleep in there.

Kane Wakeling (7)
Holy Trinity Lamorbey CE Primary School, Sidcup

Volcano Candy!

There was once a volcano.
A volcano? Yes, a volcano!
And it was large, bigger than a house,
Yes bigger than a house
What's bigger than a house?
It's just that... a volcano!

It was finally over, all over, yes,
finally all over and this happened
A candy land was built!
A candy land? Yes, a candy land
A candy land was built and it was fun!

There were so many sweets to choose from
Too many sweets to choose from
So there were candy explosions!

Olivia Ferdinand-Brown (8)
Holy Trinity Lamorbey CE Primary School, Sidcup

The Places Of Space

Haiku poetry

Space, full of bright stars,
Impossible vast, empty,
Lots of galaxies.

Space is nothingness,
It's a black velvet curtain,
Keeping light away.

Aliens lurking,
Ready to pounce, to kill us,
To devour us.

Gaze up into space,
Constellations emblazoned,
On the dark night sky.

Look! The moon and stars!
Space stations and satellites,
All orbiting Earth.

Huge rocky planets,
Orbit gargantuan stars,
Large lifeless wastelands.

The sun blazing hot,
Uranus and its large tilt,
Saturn and its rings.

Venus! Hot acid rain,
Earth and its beautiful life,
Mars with volcanoes.

Whoosh! Comets gliding,
Asteroids cause desolation,
Meteors crashing.

Space, blacker than coal,
Has no air for us to breathe,
Space is emptiness.

Oliver Samuel Drury (9)
Holy Trinity Lamorbey CE Primary School, Sidcup

Space

The moon is nature's clock,
even though it is made of rock,
The sun is like Mother Nature
that tells us to awaken,
The sun is the king
and the planets are the crown jewels,
The stars are little suns dancing
and giggling in space,
The shooting stars are racing home,
passing the planets,
Sunbathing on Venus is like lava
erupting from a volcano,
Saturn's ring is like a Frisbee,
If you go to space, don't go the Milky Way,
Otherwise, you will get coated in chocolate!

Freddie Bell (10)
Holy Trinity Lamorbey CE Primary School, Sidcup

Sinbad's Wonderland

S oon enough, Sinbad bought a boat
I n the dealer's hands was the money
N astily, the man grinned
B laring out his yellow teeth
A nxiously, Sinbad raised his eyebrows
D ancing, the dealer ran off, jumping
S adly, Sinbad left his beloved home behind

W ith fear of what would happen
O n the journey, he met some friends
N athan, Abdul, Ali and James
D efinitely, they would all become best friends
E nglish most of them, others Sri Lankan
R unning up and down the boat
"L and ahoy! Land ahoy!" Sinbad shouted
A ll of them jumped out except Ali
N one of them realised what was behind
D own went the ship and down went Ali.

Harry Benson (11)
Holy Trinity Lamorbey CE Primary School, Sidcup

All About My Family

I have a great family,
Us children go to Holy Trinity Lamorbey,
We all like cheese and crackers,
our favourite snack.
We share and care and we once flew in the air,
We had fun, we didn't care, then it came to an end,
And then we were on the ground watching TV,
playing secret agents and running around,
Then it was dinner time,
for a drink it was lemon-lime,
For food is was fish and chips,
my favourite food,
That is the end of my family rhyme.

Jethro Nanjo (7)
Holy Trinity Lamorbey CE Primary School, Sidcup

Sinbad's Wonderland

S inbad was a courageous sailor
I deas filled his head but
N ever had he ever thought of something so incredible
B ut his ideas were the best
A nd his adventure commenced
D arkness had fallen and he was in bed
S tanding in front of him was a phosphorescent mountain made of confectionary

W hy was he sleeping on a transparent candyfloss cloud?
O ver the sweet mountains he flew
N ever had he ever seen something so new
D ogrittos were everywhere
E ating all the scrumptious food
R ipe fruits were blooming
L ying on the minty ground
A nd then he came back down
N ow he was in his comfy bed
D reams filled his head.

Kate Smith (11)
Holy Trinity Lamorbey CE Primary School, Sidcup

A Journey To Space

Space is a magnificent magnet,
attracting all darkness.

The planets that race around the ball of fire,
are faster than any living creature.

When you sleep in space,
you dream of a wondrous race.

Our very own moon,
it controls the waves,
hides in our days,
and it brightens up the night,
but it doesn't make its own light.

When you get to Mars,
you can see the stars.

The moon is a guardian,
so kind, watching over us sleeping tight.

The moon is a sun catcher,
that reflects the light of the sun onto the cloudy
blue and green ball.

The moon shines bright in the sky like diamonds,
space is like a ball of darkness
rolling around everywhere.

Avaani Dutta (9)
Holy Trinity Lamorbey CE Primary School, Sidcup

My Magic TV

I had a magic TV and what I had to do
was just jump in
Then I went to Sonic Land
and climbed all the levels
Then I jumped to Mario Cart
Then I went into a race and I came in first place
Then I went to Platform 9¾
Then I got on the Hogwarts Express
Then I went to learn to magic a potion
Then I had a rest in the Great Hall
Then I had to go back home
on the Hogwarts Express
Then I jumped back out the telly.

Thomas Harding (8)
Holy Trinity Lamorbey CE Primary School, Sidcup

What About Space?

Space, space,
Lots of stars,
What about Mars?
It has the biggest volcano ever,
I wonder if space will last forever,
Mercury is nearest to the sun,
That planet is the smallest one,
Venus is very hot,
I don't think it rains a lot,
Earth, home to all people,
With all of God's steeples,
Uranus, very blue,
Have astronauts been there too?
Saturn with its big bold ring,
That's what makes it go *bling, bling!*
Neptune has the name of a god,
The god of seas and all ocean pods,
Jupiter is the one with the big storm,
Does it disappear at dawn?
Uh oh! We forgot about Pluto,
They're the planets you need to know.

Hetty Harrison (9)
Holy Trinity Lamorbey CE Primary School, Sidcup

Bluebirds

Bluebirds in the tree,
Bluebirds around me,
I love them very much,
They have a magical touch,
An angry wizard once came
and took the birds away,
The bluebirds were sad because
they didn't have a say,
The wizard gave the birds an apple,
But they thought it was a pineapple,
When I got the birds back, the wizard turned black,
I'd saved the day and the birds shouted, "Hooray!"

Ellie Shaw (8)
Holy Trinity Lamorbey CE Primary School, Sidcup

The Special Solar System

Earth is the place we live,
And we construct technological things,
Stars look even bigger on Mars,
And the planets run round the sun,
On the moon, there are holes made by moles,
And in space, they're having a race,
On Mars, we could live,
Is this all we can give?
All the stars in the sky,
Are little bulbs of hope,
Uranus lies the other way,
While we're living to this day,
Jupiter's biggest moon is Titan,
You can see it clearly in Brighton,
Jupiter is a gas giant,
And has a special diet,
Saturn is so brightly big,
And its rings are small stars,
Pluto has been rejected,
From the council of the universe.

Archie Lee Downton (9)
Holy Trinity Lamorbey CE Primary School, Sidcup

The Fantastic Moon

The planets are big
as ever, they fly around.

The astronauts fly to
Mars to see the
fantastic stars.

The black holes
cover the sleepy
space moles.

The comets fly
around watching
people all day.

Life on
Earth is very
fun and it's
full of what
we need so we
are very pleased.

The meteors look like
massive meatballs.

The rockets fly high
to the sky.

The planets are very
clever, they spin on
their own.

The sun is bright, it has
good light.

The darkness shines
everywhere, it's very
big and never
ends.

Sam Jackson (9)
Holy Trinity Lamorbey CE Primary School, Sidcup

If I Were A...

If I were a monkey, I would see some big
green bananas for me to eat.
If I were a spider, I would see my white spiderweb
as white as a ball of wool.
If I were a sloth, I would see
the big brown tree trunks.
If I were a snake, I would hear the wind
blowing in the distance.
If I were a fox, I would hear the birds
tweeting from above.
If I were a cheetah, I would hear the foxes hunting.
If I were a bird, I would feel my wings flapping.
If I were a cheetah, I would feel the grass.
if I were a bird, I would smell the flowers.
If I were a sloth, I would smell the leaves.
If I were a cheetah, I would smell
the other animals.

Ava Spooner (8)
Holy Trinity Lamorbey CE Primary School, Sidcup

Space

As you stare up to the sparkling sky,
you must quickly say goodbye,
to the Earth that you are on,
because soon, you'll be gone
to the dark, dark mass above,
away from the things you love.

You quickly spot a big black hole,
it is like a big round bowl,
as you fall towards its gloomy depths,
you realise there's only one thing left,
sprinting towards the escape pod,
you realise there's something odd,
the black hole isn't sucking you in,
but you are flying back to Earth!

And you start waving with mirth,
as you realise you're in bed,
you start to lift up your droopy head!

Albert Charles Paskins (9)
Holy Trinity Lamorbey CE Primary School, Sidcup

The Solar System

When I was flying in the sky,
I was eating all my pie.
All the stars were so bright,
making the whole place so light.
Flying, flying so, so fast,
I was having such a blast.
I was flying so, so high and
all the aliens waved bye-bye.
Passing places very fast,
I thought my ship was first class.
All of the guys were surprised,
thinking I was lying.
I passed the sun.
I passed Mercury.
I passed Venus.
I passed the Earth.
I passed Mars.
I passed Jupiter.
I passed Saturn.
I passed Uranus.

When I passed the solar system,
I got a good feeling.
I was the first man to pass the solar system!

Josephus Nanjo (9)
Holy Trinity Lamorbey CE Primary School, Sidcup

Fruity Wonderland

Never had I ever seen a bird so beautifully clean,
It picked me up and off we flew
to a land we never knew,
Above the clouds we went,
until we landed in a tent,
Full of lots of fruit which looked ever so cute,
The trees were full of cheese
and the water was full of jelly,
I hopped like a frog and landed on a log,
Then a little strawberry looked up at me
with a little bit of glee,
And as I looked up, I saw a racodile
which looked awfully like a crocodile,
It came towards me very dangerously
and picked up the strawberry
and threw it across the jelly,
It landed with a thud in a pile of mud!

Lewis James Farrow (11)
Holy Trinity Lamorbey CE Primary School, Sidcup

Animal Meals

I saw a cat, it was fat
It was eating some big rats
And then a bat ate the cat
Who ate the rats
But then a bird caught the bat
And then its babies had a feast
But then a seagull caught the birds
And ate them bit by bit
But then a whale came along
And ate the seagull and its family
Lastly, a giant came out of nowhere
And ate everything!

Sam Morgan (7)
Holy Trinity Lamorbey CE Primary School, Sidcup

Sinbad's Journey

S inbad wakes up to the noise of a beautiful peacock
I n the jungle of ferocious animals
N ever scared of the evil gorilla
B uddy is Sinbad's best friend
A dventurous Buddy is so amazing
D estroying any obstacle in their way
S unny skies on a rainy day

J ogging up Adam's Peak
O h, their adventure is sensational
U nder the water is a scary wet shark
R ain is pouring down on adventurous Buddy
N ice as a rabbit, the shark gives a wave
E verlasting adventures
Y ou can see butterflies in the sky.

Isatu Barrie (10)
Holy Trinity Lamorbey CE Primary School, Sidcup

Space Race

Today, stars, black holes and planets gather round,
To see the race of a lifetime, crikey what a sound!

All the planets getting their running tops
in record time,
Going over to the intergalactic washing line.

The crowds just keep on singing,
Hoping their team is winning.

Just like roaring lions,
Sounding just like sirens.

The sun has shot the gun,
That means it's time to have fun!

Jupiter's going like a fidget spinner,
This must mean he's a sure winner.

Only 365 days to go, Earth,
You will make it soon enough.

Benedict Keeley (10)
Holy Trinity Lamorbey CE Primary School, Sidcup

In The Forest

If I were a panther, I would see a sloth
sleeping on a tree trunk,
I would smell the rich aromas
of the fresh coconuts,
I would hear howler monkeys
howling in the moonlight,
I would feel the smooth gorillas.

If I were a sloth, I would be clinging to branches,
I would smell damp leaves dripping on my head,
I would see leopards hunting armadillos,
I would hear the roar of panthers.

If I were a spider, I would see
anacondas on the ground,
I would hear the crickets,
I would smell the juicy pineapples,
I would feel the dusty ground.

Freddie Grange (9)
Holy Trinity Lamorbey CE Primary School, Sidcup

My Goblin Friend

My goblin chased me around the house
with a mouse,
He was green but very, very keen,
I don't know why he had a sack of spears,
He ran across the tables and had my TV cables,
He drove a silver space car, he went very, very far,
He went to Mars so that was why
meteors kept on crashing into my house,
Most of the time, he went crazy
because he wasn't lazy.

Teddy Brient (8)
Holy Trinity Lamorbey CE Primary School, Sidcup

Waterfall

W *oosh!* I could hear the sound of water falling off the cliff.
A bove me, I could see white fluffy clouds in the clear blue sky.
T all trees gazed over me.
E ggs in nests in tall thick trees.
R uby-red berries bloomed in the red-hot sun.
F ascinating fishes swam gracefully in the deep blue sea.
A ll under my feet, I could feel rigid rocks piercing my feet.
L istening carefully, I could hear the trees swaying in the wind.
L ittle drops of rain fell from the sky into the carnivorous ocean.

Jada Annan (11)
Holy Trinity Lamorbey CE Primary School, Sidcup

Walking In A Summer Wonderland

As the summer evening settled down,
A beam of light cleared my frown,
Emerald-green came from the sky,
As birds flew by,
Before they landed on the ground.

To my left, I saw an overweight banana eater,
His name was Peter,
He munched and munched and munched,
Then I heard a sickening crunch!
He was a fascinating creature.

I then saw a flying rainbow above me,
She then landed on my knee,
She copied everything I said,
And she had a very funny-shaped head,
She then flew off to carry on her journey.

Grace Stewart (10)
Holy Trinity Lamorbey CE Primary School, Sidcup

Carnival

When I arrived at the carnival,
all that I could see,
were some of the samba players,
the dancers and me.

I strolled round the parade,
and then I looked around,
then suddenly, out of nowhere,
I heard the samba sounds.

I walked up to one of the dancers,
she looked very pretty,
she exclaimed, "Please, come and join me!"
and I responded, "Yippee!"

I climbed up on an elephant,
as high as the sky,
then waved to everybody,
and then I said goodbye.

Lisa Nyandusi (9)
Holy Trinity Lamorbey CE Primary School, Sidcup

A Sloth's Life

I if I were a sloth, I would sleep all day,
But I wouldn't sleep that much
because hunters might kill me midday.

If I were a sloth, my name would be Tough,
My parents would love that name
because I'd be ever so rough.

My sister would exercise,
but I wouldn't do it that much anyway,
But when I did it, I would be okay.

I would try to stay as far
as I could away from deforestation,
As humans would try to kill me,
If I heard a noise, I'd know what it would be...

Valentina Hin (8)
Holy Trinity Lamorbey CE Primary School, Sidcup

Our Never-Ending Solar System

When I look at the moon,
The world is full of gloom,
I feel like it's a giant ball.

When I look at the shining stars,
I wonder how far they go,
Travelling through our solar system.

When I set off in my rocket,
I feel myself in shock,
I never thought I'd be there!

The black holes in space,
Make me feel in place,
A never-ending night.

The astronauts, full of fear,
The crowds starting to cheer,
Thank you world for being here.

Holly Lucy Evens (9)
Holy Trinity Lamorbey CE Primary School, Sidcup

Rockety Rockets

The rockets go up and up with no destination
except the darkness with a big engine.
Aliens are strange, the rocket is big,
with lots of comets flying past it.
The aliens are unknown with lots of clones.
The moon is like cheese, lots please.
Aliens whizz through the galaxies,
if I went that fast, I'd vomit on a comet.
Life is endless like the Earth with lots of things
that orbit the great blue marble.
When I look at Earth,
all I can think about is a great ball of water.

George Panter (9)
Holy Trinity Lamorbey CE Primary School, Sidcup

The Valley Of Diamonds

Gems!
Diamonds everywhere.
To ignore them, I could not bear.
Quick as a flash, one by one
I picked them up and I was done.
To my surprise, I wasn't! What happened
wasn't pleasant. A piece of mutton fell onto my
button. Then after that, I went *splat!*
Another enormous piece of mutton fell
onto me, I wasn't full of
glee. I woke up in a
nest. I wasn't looking my
best. The mutton was
all I could see.
What was happening
to me?

Damilare Oshin (10)
Holy Trinity Lamorbey CE Primary School, Sidcup

Shipwrecked

As the nights went on and the days went by,
Rainbows were rolling in the sky,
I thought I heard an owl hoot,
Or was it something tugging at my boots?
Whoosh! Like a leopard in the sky,
Something loomed past my eyes,
As I opened a curtain of vegetation,
I was welcomed by a tingling sensation,
A phenomenal sensation struck my mind,
I thanked my god for being so kind,
Oh, what evil could have befallen us all,
If this island was instead my downfall.

Sinclair Dikeocha (11)
Holy Trinity Lamorbey CE Primary School, Sidcup

Calling Me

As I saw a fuzzy figure
That tickled my finger
I heard a roar
And saw an apple core
Something yellow and black
I thought it was a sack
As I trembled in fear
What I did hear
Was exciting
A fighting
Scene
Up in the sky
I said goodbye
I started to say hi
What I did hear up high?
A waterfall
Just like a call
Calling me and I did fall
I finally
But sadly

Said goodbye
Until next time I saw it and said hi.

Magda Augustowska (11)
Holy Trinity Lamorbey CE Primary School, Sidcup

Silly Snowfall!

There is a man in the snow,
oh, how his cheeks glow,
he walks and he dances,
he jumps and he prances,
he is falling down the hill, oh no!

There is now a white polar bear,
oh my, this one must be rare,
grey and black,
he may soon lose his hat,
it has run away right over there!

Fluffy clouds in the blue sky,
on them, he wants to lie,
white and puffy,
his nose is kind of stuffy,
If he is hiding, does that make him shy?

Sophie Scanlon (11)
Holy Trinity Lamorbey CE Primary School, Sidcup

The Wild Wonderful Carnival

Colourful wacky masks fill the city with joy,
giant creative floats attract people
to their wonders,
excited Brazilians munch up all the delicious food,
bright amazing paints make everybody's skin
look like a rainbow.

The really loud samba music pushes the tempo up,
magnificent magical dancers
create wildness everywhere,
beautiful Brazilian flags sway from side to side,
the scorching flaming sun sets the city on fire.

Percy Cavanagh (9)
Holy Trinity Lamorbey CE Primary School, Sidcup

Opposite World

Opposite World is a secret world that nobody knows about except you and me. This world will blow your mind. In the blink of an eye, you will be in this world but only if you believe. It has black and white unicorns, black and white rainbows, colourful skies and candyfloss clouds which are obviously rainbow-coloured, animals going to school, us living outside. Believe and it will be so true.

Fola Edgal (8)
Holy Trinity Lamorbey CE Primary School, Sidcup

Sinbad's Wonderland

As I crept,
I had to leap,
my feet,
suddenly touched a leaf.

I smiled with glee,
as my reflection stared back at me,
as a bird swooped,
and loop the looped.

The flowers bloomed,
like 1000 balloons,
a leopard appeared,
it was getting very near!

A marvellous zebra came,
why would anybody complain?
Roar! Grr!
the leopard went
as he twisted his head...

Daisy Meir (10)
Holy Trinity Lamorbey CE Primary School, Sidcup

When I Look Up

When I look up at the sun,
The day has just begun,
I want to have some fun.

When I look at the moon,
The stars are in full bloom
I think it must be bedtime soon.

When I look at the biggest brightest stars,
The shimmery gems from afar,
I wonder what they all really are.

When I look at our planet, Earth,
The thousands of pounds it must be worth,
I wonder when it had its birth.

Emily Frowde (10)
Holy Trinity Lamorbey CE Primary School, Sidcup

Sinbad's Wonderland

The golden ball that leapt to the sky,
Shone in silence as the day went by.
The inexplicable smell of the heat,
Shot up my nose within a heartbeat.

Drip, drip, drip, drip,
The crystal droplets on my lip.
As the droplets hit the ground,
Their tiny faces turned to frowns.

And as if within a blink,
The sun began to sink.
The sky turned black and clear,
Darkness was here.

Isobella Dixon (11)
Holy Trinity Lamorbey CE Primary School, Sidcup

The Wonderland

The towering trees,
covered the sky,
not a speck of light,
hit my eye.

The rippling waves,
rushed like bolts of lightning,
my body clenched, tightening.

A fuzzy, frantic figure,
lurked behind me,
swinging freely,
hanging on a tree.

The lovely fresh air was coming closer,
as I took a step closer,
it was like a fresh breath of air,
combing through my hair.

Lucy Sullivan (11)
Holy Trinity Lamorbey CE Primary School, Sidcup

The Hummingbird

Whoosh!
Colour grenades hit the trees around me,
Forming beautiful shapes about the size of bees,
With long thin mouths and tails like fans,
This place was different, unlike London,
It wasn't littered with cans,
Shrieking rang out through the air,
Echo, echo! It was coming from its lair,
Its claws were sharp and raking,
They were so heavy, you could hear twigs breaking.

Elliot Martin (11)
Holy Trinity Lamorbey CE Primary School, Sidcup

Sinbad In A Summer Wonderland!

The ripples of the water,
Were shiny and deep.
As a pocket-sized creature,
With two measly wings flew past me.

Like a knot in my lace,
The vines were carelessly dangling.
I could smell its healthy perfume,
And hear the birds singing.

Splash, splash the waterfall went.
The crystal-clear water,
Were making me quiver.
What a beautiful sight this really was!

Macie Alana Davey (11)
Holy Trinity Lamorbey CE Primary School, Sidcup

If I Were A Crocodile...

If I were a crocodile, I would have sharp teeth.
If I were a crocodile, I would have green feet.
If I were a crocodile, I would swim all day.
If I were a crocodile, I would like to play.
If I were a crocodile, I would hunt some fish.
If I were a crocodile, my tail would always swish.

Eva Wells (9)
Holy Trinity Lamorbey CE Primary School, Sidcup

The Dragon Egg

Far away is a weird wacky land,
with unicorns and giraffes playing in the sand.
There's also an egg that was made by a dragon,
it's spotty, it's furry and it's pushed in a wagon.
Soon it will hatch such a wonderful sight,
it will fill up the world with a big shining light!
Sometimes the egg moves
And sometimes the egg cracks,
sometimes the egg is chased by the wild cats.

Ava Green (8)
Holy Trinity Lamorbey CE Primary School, Sidcup

That Jumping Monkey!

That day I was a monkey...
I could see everything from far
And near and near and far,
I could jump from tree to tree
And that's how I did see,
I could hear so much,
I could even hear my own type of bunch,
I loved to eat bananas,
I just loved to smell fresh bananas!
My tree was my home tree,
When it shook, I looked down,
And there was a stupid, slithering, old snake!

Holly Highmore (9)
Holy Trinity Lamorbey CE Primary School, Sidcup

My Colourful Creatures

Whoosh!
Colours whizzed around me,
Like rainbows dancing about,
Bright bombs of colour were all I could see.

Shrieks filled the noiseless air,
Like echoes from their lair,
Their deafening calls killed my ears,
Filling me with deep, dark fears.

Leaving their feathers,
Like pieces of leather,
They rapidly scattered away,
Saying goodbye for the day.

Chloe Louise Wing Yan Tse (10)
Holy Trinity Lamorbey CE Primary School, Sidcup

Black Panther

Deep down in the forest,
all of the animals have a rainy rest.

But there is a big fright,
during the night.

There is an animal,
it isn't a camel.

He lives in the shadows,
while the other animals live in the meadows.

Before he goes to sleep,
he does a quick leap.

He is the black panther,
he's so scary, he will make you pant.

Munachiso Onyeanusi (8)
Holy Trinity Lamorbey CE Primary School, Sidcup

Space

S tars flying across the sky while people watch the vast ocean sky with swarms of meteorites destined to destroy our lives.
P lanets spinning with momentum while Pluto floats for freedom.
A stronauts and NASA see the world, while the rest love eating Twirls.
C omets fly through outer space while we watch in grace.
E arth has had lots of bangs from asteroids having fun.

Theodore Andreas Georgiou (10)
Holy Trinity Lamorbey CE Primary School, Sidcup

Space

Space is a face, staring down on Earth,
watching down with a bird's eye view.

Space is full of grace,
lonely lying above the cloudy blue sky.

Space is a race, so you can be the first.
As you watch the sky,
you hope you can conquer space one day.

Space is a place waiting for mysteries to be solved.

Space is ace, like the highest in cards.

Harry Beerling (9)
Holy Trinity Lamorbey CE Primary School, Sidcup

Weird Wonders!

W hat is this land I have found?
O ranges like hearts, not round!
N ever have I seen this before
D ancing flowers that I adore,
E very type there can be.
R acing cars in the sea?
L ollipops as doors,
A nd it just gets mad, more and more!
N o one in this land seems mean...
D ear me, that was a funny dream!

Grace Foden (11)
Holy Trinity Lamorbey CE Primary School, Sidcup

The Rainforest Animals

If I were a spider, what would I see?
Grass, ants and jaguars racing.

If I were a piranha, what would I hear?
Piranhas wagging their tails
And eating people alive.

If I were a jumping spider, what would I smell?
I would smell my toxic web and leaves.

If I were a panther, what would I feel?
I'd feel the furious wind and rain on my fur.

Dami Olofinlua (8)
Holy Trinity Lamorbey CE Primary School, Sidcup

The Mermaid Scream

I heard a mermaid scream
It made me want ice cream
I thought she wanted it too
But instead, I got her a shoe
She only had a fin
So I put the shoe in the bin
It made me very angry
So I just got her a cranberry
She loved it very much
But then a wicked witch came
And took her to her hutch
Then I got her back again
She was very happy again!

Grace Elouise Shaw (8)
Holy Trinity Lamorbey CE Primary School, Sidcup

The Life Of The Sloth!

If I were a sloth, I could see the
great big blue sky above me.

If I were a sloth, I could hear the
sweet tweeting birds while meeting their friends.

If I were a sloth I could smell the
damp leaves while trying to nap.

If I were a sloth I could feel the
scratching on the trees I would be sitting on
while patching up my fur with moss.

Eimear O'Mahony (8)
Holy Trinity Lamorbey CE Primary School, Sidcup

Trees Of Different Types And Not Bushes

Some are big, some are small
Some are large, some are thin
Some are twisted, some are not
Some are bendy, some are not
Some are yellow and some are green
All sorts of different colours
Some have cherries, some have apples
Some are short and some are tall
As long as they're all trees
Not bushes
No bushes allowed
In the tree poem!

Blake McIntosh (7)
Holy Trinity Lamorbey CE Primary School, Sidcup

Ant

If I were a microscopic ant,
I would smell and feel the green grass
and the brown dirt always touching my legs.
The grass would be as green and as smooth
as a green book and the dirt
would be as smooth as a blanket.
I would see trees, dirt and other animals.

Luke Hutchins (8)
Holy Trinity Lamorbey CE Primary School, Sidcup

Rainforest

As the sunny sun rises,
A little fly flies,
As the monkeys climb out,
They decide to climb the mount,
When the animal parents wake up,
The kids have gone to the dump,
As the humans have a parade,
The sloth runs away,
As the water smells fresh,
The humans make a mess,
As the animals have a feast,
There are lots of wild beasts.

Eleanor-Rose Delaney (9)
Holy Trinity Lamorbey CE Primary School, Sidcup

Deep In The Forest

Deep in the rainforest,
Lives Borris,
The most cheekiest animal in the land,
And he will jump on you if he can.

Deep in the jungle,
Lives Bumble,
The smallest animal in the place,
And he gets away from the hunting chase.

Through the rainforest,
Is Horris,
This snake is so slippery,
He moves so slitheringly.

Abdulmuqeet Sulaimon (8)
Holy Trinity Lamorbey CE Primary School, Sidcup

Amazon Rainforest Creatures

There are pink dolphins swimming, feeling free, their scales are gleaming in the sunlight.
The lions roar, shaking their paws ferociously.
The monkeys claw ruthlessly, shaking their paws.
The jaguar's whole body is shaking
like Mount Sugarloaf.
The fearless birds are peacefully flapping their wings while the ferocious lions are napping.

Joshua Walters (9)
Holy Trinity Lamorbey CE Primary School, Sidcup

Rainforest Danger

If I were a panther, I would see my prey,
If I were a piranha, I would smell saltwater,
If I were a sloth, I would hear jaguars
pouncing below me,
If I were a scorpion, I would feel fresh leaves,
If I were a jaguar, I would smell animals' dung,
If I were a snake, I would see dark shadowy shapes
moving towards me in the dark.

Isabelle Harding (9)
Holy Trinity Lamorbey CE Primary School, Sidcup

The Amazon Rainforest

If I were a cheetah, I would run like the wind.
If I were a monkey, I would climb the trees.
If I were a cheetah, I would catch my prey.
If I were a monkey, I would not let them catch me.
If I were a bug, I would climb the trees.
If I were a bug, I would fly everywhere.
If I were a bee, I would fly everywhere
In the rainforest.

Albie King (8)
Holy Trinity Lamorbey CE Primary School, Sidcup

Imagination In The Rainforest

Imagine being a spider looking at blurriness,
Imagine listening to leaves
getting crushed all day long,
Imagine smelling the dirtiness of the river,
Imagine being a jaguar
getting scratched from branches,
Imagine birds singing beautifully,
Imagine the smell of trees,
Imagine living there,
Imagine a world like that.

Ivy Lee (9)
Holy Trinity Lamorbey CE Primary School, Sidcup

Space

S hining stars soaring through meteorites in the Milky Way, deep in space.
T eam NASA (National Astronaut Space Academy) helping the US win the race.
A liens, the multi-legged creatures that are UFO pilot aces.
R ockets soaring through the vast oceans of space.
S aturn is a planet in the wondrous solar system.

Harry George (9)
Holy Trinity Lamorbey CE Primary School, Sidcup

Space Rhyme

Space is a place
where you can explore far and wide.
Scientists believe that the planets
are unable to hide.
Jupiter is the largest planet and it's hard to beat.
Saturn is getting bigger,
it must have had something to eat!
The solar system is where you look to see the stars.
It's like eating Mars bars.

Joel Unger (9)
Holy Trinity Lamorbey CE Primary School, Sidcup

The Space Person

I want to explore space,
discovering all its secrets,
wiggling around the worlds of wonders,
listening to the beat of my heart.

I am staring in wonder,
at the little streets below,
wondering how I got up here!

I am running around,
half out of my mind,
hoping to go back to the world below.

Charlie Workman (9)
Holy Trinity Lamorbey CE Primary School, Sidcup

The Fortunes Of Sinbad

S unny sun, shivering Sinbad
I maginative, ignorant, innocent, imbecile
N aught Sinbad running as fast as a flash because of a lion
B est friends having an underwater BBQ
A mazing party until a dragon robot destroys the party
D angerous ice cream waterfall heading to the desert.

Abdulmateen Sulaimon (10)
Holy Trinity Lamorbey CE Primary School, Sidcup

Being A Sailor In Monster Land

Being a sailor makes life tough,
getting attacked by the Loch Ness Monster and stuff.
When ashore, please take care,
a Cyclops might come and rip off your hair.

Well, back to the boat;
You're in a king's moat;
Being chased by a candy whale,
that's being ridden by a tiny snail.

Shaun Miles (11)
Holy Trinity Lamorbey CE Primary School, Sidcup

The Moonlight

The sun has gone, the night has come,
now the moonlight shines.
I walk outside to see my tree,
and when I come here, I always feel free.
I can see the fireflies fly,
as they light up the sky.
I can see the moonlight,
because it is so bright.
Now I'll go to bed,
to rest my head.

Emma Anthony (8)
Holy Trinity Lamorbey CE Primary School, Sidcup

Pizza

Pizza, I love pizza
Pizza is incredible
Pizza is Italian food
It's my favourite food
Mmm it smells so good
Very good
I can't stop eating at one bit
I have pizza every day non-stop
And now some's ready and yummy
Have you had pizza
Or been to Pizza Express?

Poppy Back (7)
Holy Trinity Lamorbey CE Primary School, Sidcup

Tiger

If I were a tiger, I would hunt for food.
If I were a tiger, I would be a real cool dude.
If I were a tiger, I would look after my cubs.
If I were a tiger, I wouldn't eat bugs.
If I were a tiger, I would live in the rainforest.
If I were a tiger, I would have a wife named Doris.

James Dixon (9)
Holy Trinity Lamorbey CE Primary School, Sidcup

If I Were A Tiger

If I were a tiger, I would use my claws to hunt prey.
If I were a tiger, I would be lazy and sleep all day.
If I were a tiger, I would hide in the trees.
If I were a tiger, I would have little cubs to tease.
If I were at tiger, I would growl.
If I were a tiger, I would be loud.

Zara Eleanor Lin Heyburn (8)
Holy Trinity Lamorbey CE Primary School, Sidcup

Galaxies

The colours of the rainbow
Blue, purple, pink
They flash and change
In a wink
The colours are like unicorns
The stars a deep gold like their horns
While I listen
They shine and glisten
And I hear
The sound of nothing
And I see colours dancing.

Katherine Childs (10)
Holy Trinity Lamorbey CE Primary School, Sidcup

Candy Land!

Have you ever dreamt of a world full of candy?
Well, here you are, wandering about,
While eating sweets that are flying around,
Waterfalls of chocolate,
And clouds made out of cotton candy,
And a sun made out of a sugary lemon,
And infinite coloured rainbows.

Amaya Vongswang (9)
Holy Trinity Lamorbey CE Primary School, Sidcup

Gallons Of Animals

Brazil is the fifth biggest country
with lots of monkeys,
If I were a cheetah, I would pounce on my prey
but if an elephant came, I would run away,
If I shook some trees, I would find a lot of bees,
If you like the rainforest,
you would like rainy countries.

Semilore Akinfe (8)
Holy Trinity Lamorbey CE Primary School, Sidcup

What Sinbad Sees

Monkeys swinging through the trees
Crawling ants and buzzing bees
Clear skies and glass-like seas
This is what Sinbad sees.

A meek dragon come to heed
A bench that makes your bottom bleed
A goat that flies in the sky
This is what Sinbad sees.

Aoife Reilly (11)
Holy Trinity Lamorbey CE Primary School, Sidcup

Magical Rainforest

If I were a crocodile,
I would hear waves crashing
And waterfalls flowing.
If I were a panther,
I would see sloths sleeping and macaws flying.
But I'd just love the rainforest!

Daisy Macangus (8)
Holy Trinity Lamorbey CE Primary School, Sidcup

Peter The Banana Eater!

To my left, I saw a big brown banana eater,
His name was Peter,
He also was a meat eater,
He munched and munched,
Until he heard a big crunch,
To know that he'd eaten
The most famous banana bunch,
And then he finished off his lunch.

Chloe Ella Parr (10)
Holy Trinity Lamorbey CE Primary School, Sidcup

Supersonic Astronaut

When I grow up, I wish to be an astronaut,
An astronaut who travels through space,
Inside my glittering grey rocket,
I will put my hand in my pocket
and pull out a locket,
And I shall spend ages
weaving through the amazing planets.

Georgie Stanley McMahon (10)
Holy Trinity Lamorbey CE Primary School, Sidcup

Slithery Snake

If I were a snake,
I would put out my bait,
I'd slither and wait,
Till my dinner came,
Slowly and carefully,
I'd smack them quick,
You would hear them screaming,
And I'd eat them quick.

Lucas Kai Davids-Ruiz (8)
Holy Trinity Lamorbey CE Primary School, Sidcup

The Rainforest Poem

If I were a sloth,
I would move so slowly and see massive trees,
And I would hear not a lot of things,
I would smell the wet leaves drifting up my nose,
I would feel the bark of the trees.

Pagan Honeywell (9)
Holy Trinity Lamorbey CE Primary School, Sidcup

Jungle

I saw a monkey in a tree
He was drinking a cup of tea
A big elephant stomped in the mud
Its foot made a great big thud
The monkey jumped up very high
He landed in a banana pie.

Stanley Swan (8)
Holy Trinity Lamorbey CE Primary School, Sidcup

About The Rainforest

I can hear wind coming in my ear
I can see trees and leaves on the floor
I can feel the trees' branches
I can smell plants and animals.

Jermaine Annan (8)
Holy Trinity Lamorbey CE Primary School, Sidcup

Skiing

A haiku

Skiing is scary,
Down a mountain, very fast
And I'm never last.

Freddie Palmer (9)
Holy Trinity Lamorbey CE Primary School, Sidcup

The Lazy Lupungos

I have a lazy Lupungos,
Who has a big fungus,
He is lazy all day,
But he talks to his friend, Ray,
He lies in a gigantic crib,
But wears a tiny bib!

I have a lazy Lupungos,
Who has a big fungus,
He's on his phone all night,
Until he gets a big fright,
He's always on his device,
As well as eating rice!

I have a lazy Lupungos,
Who has a big fungus,
He doesn't socialise at lunchtime,
And he doesn't like to rhyme,
When he has a break,
He always has some cake!

Reuben Yves-Louis Mundell (9)
Jubilee Primary School, Maidstone

I Slept In A Bathtub

I slept in a bathtub,
It was cold,
I realised I was bald.

I slept in a bathtub,
I had teddies,
After that, I put on wellies.

I slept in a bathtub,
I flew in it,
Seconds later, I grew in it.

I slept in a bathtub,
I met Fred,
Years later, I built a bed.

I slept in a bathtub,
I was sleepy,
Hours later, it was creepy.

Thomas Hugo-Ross Mundell (8)
Jubilee Primary School, Maidstone

My Underwater BBQ Didn't Go To Plan

My underwater BBQ didn't go to plan,
It started when the octopus stole the frying pan.
Then came along the lobster,
Who pinched the cooking tongs.
Then appeared the barracudas,
Who started singing songs.
The prawns were misbehaving,
They were dancing with the squid.
The dolphins and the whales kept,
Unscrewing the ketchup lid.
I carried on regardless,
To cook my favourite dish.
But soon, they were all looking at me,
Because I was cooking fish!

Nathan Molloy (9)
Jubilee Primary School, Maidstone

I Am Surfing In The Loo

Smelly, dirty, wet
How I wish I had become a vet
To, to, to plain and wet
But I am a surfer, a surfer
So I should just get wet.

Yes, I am surfing
In the loo!
It may sound weird
But you are too.
It is like the sea and it
Smells of wee!

Oh no, someone's bum
I need to run
Flush!
Down the drain!

Poppy Schofield (9)
Jubilee Primary School, Maidstone

Lava Surfing Competition

L ava surfing competition time
A ustralian Leon goes up first
V olcano hot moves on Leon's lavaboard
A sher of France next up

S urfing the waves
U nderneath the volcano, a crowd is growing
R euben of South Africa is up last
F inishing by burning his bum
I n the crowd, the judges watch well
N ew lavaboards, a cool prize
G uess who the winner is? Leon Price!

Leon Elijah Price (9)
Jubilee Primary School, Maidstone

Learning To Speak Alien

Learning to speak alien was rather hard,
First I needed to learn the simple words,
But all I heard was *gerds, gerds, gerds!*
Then I needed to learn the colours
But all I heard was *bubbles, bubbles, bubbles!*
The special word was the easiest,
Because all it was,
Was *bos, bos, bos!*
When I got back to Earth,
All I said was *gerth, gerth, gerth!*
Why oh why did I learn to speak alien?

Eden Longley (9)
Jubilee Primary School, Maidstone

Moon Cheese!

Once I went to the moon,
I saw a little block,
It was bright yellow,
And it was as squishy as a marshmallow,
I thought it was a rock,
But then I got a shock,
An alien popped up,
Out of a little crater,
He was great, his name was Flat,
And he loved his crater,
And his crater was made of moon cheese,
But I'm never going to space again!

Ciara Katrina Denise Jane Crittall (9)
Jubilee Primary School, Maidstone

Cookie Moon

Eating all the cookies,
Getting a bit fat,
Weirdly, there are cookie aliens,
Also cookie houses,
It has a cookie shop,
It has a cookie sword,
And a cookie PlayStation,
Plus a cookie controller,
I go to the cookie mechanic,
I buy a cookie car,
Now I'm going back to Earth,
But it's hard to choose which spaceship
I should fly!

Harrison Jones (8)
Jubilee Primary School, Maidstone

Surfing On A Fruit Salad

I once went surfing on a fruit salad,
I first dodged the amazing apples,
And rode over wind-whipped watermelon waves,
Next, I frantically swam in yoghurt,
I passed powerful peaches punching,
I saw strawberries surfing,
And watching groovy grapes dancing,
I was having a lovely time,
But suddenly, I crashed my banana boat,
Into the raisin river...
It was delicious!

Ross Benjamin Price (8)
Jubilee Primary School, Maidstone

My Pet Mouse

I have a pet mouse,
And she lives in my house,
She always wears a hat,
And she loves rainbow cats,
Although she can walk,
She never talks,
Once she sat on my rainbow mat,
Then she stole my blue bobble hat,
She's sometimes keen,
She's sometimes mean,
I have a pet mouse,
And she lives in my house.

Maya Fawzy (9)
Jubilee Primary School, Maidstone

My Cake

My cake is very big with lots of wrinkles
My cake has lots of sprinkles with heavy cream
Made in my dreams
I stuff my face
With not much grace
My cake is very yummy
It makes me go funny
I eat my cate
But it took hours to bake
I love my cake
But I think this is all fake!

Neave Elliott (8)
Jubilee Primary School, Maidstone

Having A Pet Rainbow Cat

My new pet rainbow cat,
His favourite colour is red,
And his favourite object is his bed,
His favourite food is meat,
The colour of a wooden seat,
And he lives in my house,
Like an ordinary mouse!

Two days later...

Now he is very fat,
So now he sleeps on the mat,
I don't know what to call him,
So I'll call him Tim,
But now he's all crazy,
And also very lazy!

Pearl Deri Hepworth (8)
Jubilee Primary School, Maidstone

Marshmallow Clouds

Marshmallow clouds are very soft,
But suddenly, I begin to cough,
They are fluffy and sweet,
They are good to eat,
We stuff ourselves,
When we meet friendly elves,
Marshmallow clouds are very yummy,
Very yummy in my tummy!

Eulalie Sylvie Mundell (8)
Jubilee Primary School, Maidstone

Jelly

Jelly, jelly on the plate,
I just don't want to meet my fate,
Oh no, here he comes, going to bite my flesh,
But I can slide away easily because I'm fresh,
Slide, slide, sliding around, I'm gaining ground,
But now I'm embarrassed because I'm in mud.

Aryan Ahmed (8)
Jubilee Primary School, Maidstone

My Moon Party

M y moon party is starting
O h, the aliens must have arrived
O utside I run
N ow the Milky Way begins

P arty all night, party all day
A s we dance the night away
R unning and giggling
T he guests giggle and run
Y ou've never had a moon party this fun!

Haven Thandiwe Fesshaie (8)
Jubilee Primary School, Maidstone

BBQ Pig

When we have BBQs,
The BBQ pig throws out the lot,
It must contain a jetpack,
On its back,
I am sure it watches me,
I don't know what to do,
If this thing follows me,
I must watch what I do,
Just in case I do anything in front of that thing,
I now wish I had never got a BBQ.

Matthew James Rich (9)
Jubilee Primary School, Maidstone

A Train In Space

Wouldn't it be nice if you could get a train to space?
You could get there at a very fast pace,
Train stops to the moon,
And the stars would twinkle as you zoom,
You could see Mars, Mercury and Pluto too,
Even take a picnic if you choose too,
It would feel like a roller coaster
as it would go so fast,
But it would have to
if you wanted to get to Mars,
Wouldn't it be nice
if you could get a train to space?
But it's good when you
are finally back on Earth and safe.

Oliver Milchard (7)
St Peter-In-Thanet CE Junior School, St Peters

The Sizzling Sausage

The sizzling sausage leapt off my plate
Frightened me and made me late
He asked me if I wanted to dance
I said no to him, not a chance
Then he asked me out for a walk
I said, "No, sausages can't talk!"
"But I'm different, please be my friend!"
"No, you're simply just pretend."
"But here, I'm dancing, can't you see?
Please say yes and set me free
Or I'll be eaten in one big bite
Which will give me a great fright.
"Okay, fine
But look at the time
They'll be in for lunch
Munch, munch, munch!
Jump onto the chair but mind my hair!"
But the sausage landed on me,
Pinched my pants and made me pee!
"I'll push you out, but don't jump about
Until we get to the door

Get on the floor
Then you'll be free
And I can tell my friends
About the sausage that was not pretend!"

Daisy May Websper (7)
St Peter-In-Thanet CE Junior School, St Peters

A Dragon That Could Breathe Fire

A dragon could breathe fire,
He was a big liar,
His castle was haunted,
The last place you wanted,
All the bricks were burnt,
He never learnt,
He was not very nice,
He didn't eat rice,
The dragon's roar was very loud,
He was always very proud,
He could not read,
He wouldn't do a good deed,
As the bricks started to rot
They were still very hot,
He would sit around all day,
He would burn a lot of hay,
He would not listen,
Then his legs would stiffen,

He would then stay away,
From that burnt hay.

Frankie Staveley (10)
St Peter-In-Thanet CE Junior School, St Peters

Mad Hatter's Tea Party!

The Mad Hatter invited me to his tea party,
it was crazy...
The Hatter's tea was way too hot,
Dormouse was scared so hid in the teapot,
I tried to calm the crazy hare down,
But he was worried about his clock's ticking sound,
People say the Queen of Hearts is bad,
But wait till you meet Alice, she's absurd.

The Cheshire Cat's smile went from ear to ear,
But sometimes his smile turned into a sneer,
The beautiful White Queen came to visit us,
She said the Hatter was making a fuss,
But he didn't listen and just carried on,
Singing his weird little Hatter song,
"Da, da, da I'm the Hatter you see,
Da, da, da nothing can stop me!"

The Hatter carried on singing for most of the day,
In his strange 'n' special Hatter way,
I lost track of time and wanted to stay,
But suddenly found myself being whisked away,

Back home to the warmth of my cuddly sofa,
My tea party adventure was finally over!

Lilia Mai Harris (10)
St Peter-In-Thanet CE Junior School, St Peters

Rainbow

I swiped a rainbow and it turned grey,
I said that I would return the colours another day,
I came back home and turned my house purple,
When I went inside, I saw two turtles,
They were looking a bit peckish I could really see,
So I got some leaves and got my key,
Then went to the beach where I banged my knee,
Then I went to heal it in the sea,
It looked a bit grey, so I turned it blue,
But then it looked sad, so I thought pink would do,
I went back home to make a strawberry milkshake,
I didn't like the pink so I added a bit of red,
But then it turned yellow instead,
I turned my hair orange, red, then green
But it was awful,
those colours should never be seen,
I turned my hair back to blonde,
And thought the colours should go back
where they belonged,
I swiped a rainbow and it looked great,

And went back home to tell my mum,
dad and sister, Kate.

Hettie Mabel Hunt (10)
St Peter-In-Thanet CE Junior School, St Peters

Mary The Tooth Fairy

There once was a tooth fairy called Mary,
One night, she went to work
and found something very scary,
Normally, the teeth she found were nice and clean,
However, this one shocked her
and made her scream,
It was a vampire tooth!
It was black and pointy with a hole in the middle,
Mary could see where the sugar had nibbled,
She picked it up and felt a prick,
And into a vampire she turned quick,
Her fairy wings changed, she now had a cape,
Her perfect teeth started to change shape,
She was a vampire!
She visited more houses,
but instead of taking teeth,
She sucked their blood,
leaving no money beneath,
She was too busy to notice
the sun starting to appear,
She melted away

and there was no more fear,
And that was the end of Mary the tooth fairy,
And never again will we hear of Mary.

Maisie Biggs (7)
St Peter-In-Thanet CE Junior School, St Peters

The Right That Was Left But The Up That Was Down

So here we are again in the Forest of Nonsense,
Or maybe we are stuck under the sea
of Biggle Boggle Boo,
We have no questions to answer,
oh wait, we have two!
Was the right really left?
And was the up really down?
Quick, we can hear Tripper Troopers marching,
And now the purple hyenas laughing!
We need to know the answers
because the question marks are floating,
The owl is sweeping
and the cupcakes keep gloating.
Look, I can see the answers over there
by the crooked chair,
Jump on the wave of full stops,
surf through the commas and the lollipops,
At last, we have the answers,

they are here in my hand,
"Did I tell you I have 400 noses?
Now, get off my land!"

Lily Skinner (10)
St Peter-In-Thanet CE Junior School, St Peters

Sunbathing On A Cloud

I'm floating high, high up in the air,
Cuddling my teddy bear!
Nobody can stop me now,
For I am sunbathing on a cloud.
Down on the farm, I see a cow,
The clouds are moving swiftly and gently,
The sun is shining very intently -
I'd rather be here than in my Bentley!
My skin is becoming rather tanned,
All the way down to my hand.
Suddenly, my cloud starts to shake,
Although less powerful than an earthquake.
Down I come, down, down, down!
I bump and land right in my town.
Gradually, slowly, I start to frown,
I loved sunbathing on my cloud.
That feeling of being high up -
Such a peaceful sound,
Oh how I miss my comfy cloud!

Calliope Hamilton (9)
St Peter-In-Thanet CE Junior School, St Peters

Dunkirk

Us British had hope
We did not say nope
When escaping from the great antelope -
Germany
The one who didn't fight for harmony
We got picked up by our people's ships
350,000 of us
Then we went home to eat fish and chips
850 from Ramsgate they came
But all with one aim
To rescue us British
They destroyed the naval vessels
Because their bombings were successful
We got back home at the end of the day safely
Because our people acted bravely
We are British
And our country isn't yet diminished
We had a man with a plan then
Through the years, we have had people with plans
Until the day Brexit came along...

George Randall (11)
St Peter-In-Thanet CE Junior School, St Peters

The Crazy World Above!

Anything is possible as you can plainly see
Fish are flying in the sky, birds are in the sea.

The fish fly up to space and meet a green giant
Hair the colour of strawberry jam
Beard the colour of pumpkin pie
His socks are yellow, his shoes are bright
His coat and trousers are red and white.

They explore the planet and see a little frog
He is cuter than can be
He is floating on a lily pad
He says, "Come in, come swim with me!"

The fish and the frogs jump into the lake
In comes the giant, then the moon begins to quake
"Quick, hold on!" they all shout
Friends forever, they were never in doubt.

Macy Ann Martin (9)
St Peter-In-Thanet CE Junior School, St Peters

A Drink From The Goblet Of Fire

In Hogwarts hall, the young girl stepped,
The Goblet of Fire was on her left.
Around it glowed a ring of blue,
But the goblet burnt with a ruby hue.
Others might put their names in the cup,
But precocious Alice wanted to sup.
Then she remembered Dumbledore's curse,
The taste might be bad
but a beard would be worse!
She thought about names
that go round in your head,
But names in your gullet...
you might end up dead!
A quick reflection, then a better idea,
Entered the mind of our pretty young dear.
I think I'll sit down with a cup of tea,
and take a quick look at what's on TV.

Michaela Murphy (11)
St Peter-In-Thanet CE Junior School, St Peters

The Day I Surfed Down A Volcano!

Once I surfed down a volcano,
You are probably saying, 'that sounds stupid to me!'
But I say,
It's the most fun thing you could see!

If you dipped your finger in the lava,
You would probably scream,
I bet you would never want to do that,
Even in your dreams.

I got it out,
I hopped on my board,
So many people were screaming,
I couldn't be ignored!

I zoomed through the lava,
I weaved through the rocks,
People were staring at me,
In silent shock.

As I reached the bottom,
People gave me great applause,
Even the animals clapped,
With their paws!

Layla Bartlett (10)
St Peter-In-Thanet CE Junior School, St Peters

Lego Monster

He snatched and he grabbed
the helpless Lego pieces,
He connected and squashed the Lego
till he made a Lego monster,
Then suddenly... "Come down here,
sweetie! You need to Hoover!"
So he got up and slammed the door
and ran downstairs,
There was a slam and a creak
coming from the bedroom,
A snatch and a grab too,
and the Lego monster tore the room to pieces!

Thomas Pike (10)
St Peter-In-Thanet CE Junior School, St Peters

Friendship

Friendship, a thing that is like a balloon or an ant,
Very delicate and
there are a lot of twists and turns,
But in the end, it's a masterpiece,
It's very hard to explain,
You don't learn it at school,
But if you haven't learnt friendship,
You haven't learnt anything at all,
When my friend is sad,
I look after her and you should too,
That's what friendship is about,
People shouldn't love their friend for what they are,
But *who* they are,
And when you have arguments, finish,
With a great big bear hug!

Marlie-Anne McGregor (9)
St Peter-In-Thanet CE Junior School, St Peters

I Woke Up On A Whale

I woke up on a whale, I felt very pale,
It was pretty high, I thought,
this thing needs a handrail!
Trying to sleep on his back was an epic fail,
I got woken up by the flying fish
with their slippery scales,
But it was like indoor play up there,
so I slid up and down his tail,
I was trying to shout to him, but he couldn't hear,
the wind was blowing a gale,
The only way I could get home
was to retrace my trail,
So I rode on the back of a dolphin
whose name was Gareth Bale

Riley Evans (9)
St Peter-In-Thanet CE Junior School, St Peters

My Dog, Buddy

I had a little doggy and
Buddy was his name
he ate all my homework
oh, it was such a shame.

When I'd written it out
I'd left it on the shelf
but when I wasn't
looking, Buddy thought
he'd help himself.

Before I could do anything
I'd turned around and
yelled, but all I saw was
my homework in his mouth.

When I'd got my homework
back, it was chewed up in
a ball, all soggy and
I couldn't hand it in
at all.

Luke Hopson (9)
St Peter-In-Thanet CE Junior School, St Peters

Tea With Dumbledore In Space!

I knew I had met him in my dreams,
but today it really happened to me.
The lord I loved in all the films,
became visible to all mankind.
It was Dumbledore,
the man who was out of this world... literally!

He came to my muggle school
it was a dream come true.
It made me tremble
it made me shake.
He told me about space...
He took me for tea in a faraway place.
You guessed it, he took me to space!
Oh how he did it, I just don't know.

Teaghan Dooley (11)
St Peter-In-Thanet CE Junior School, St Peters

My Baby Dragon

I sew the scales to the tail of my baby dragon,
As he wakes up, he whines and wails,
But as present turns to past,
I grow slow and he grows fast,
Although, as time starts to pass,
We age,
And like my child, he goes his own way,
But after day and day,
He comes back to say,
"I have carried on your legacy,
And have stitched myself a son!"
Then, everyone in the room smiles,
Everyone.

Katherine Jenkins (10)
St Peter-In-Thanet CE Junior School, St Peters

The Candy House And The Cheese House

Mandy wanted to make a house out of candy,
The mouse wanted to make a house out of cheese,
Mandy made a house of candy,
And the mouse made a house of cheese,
The mouse used melted cheese to stick it together,
And Mandy used bubblegum to stick hers together,
But when Mandy and the mouse
tasted their own houses,
They didn't like them, so they changed houses
and lived happily ever after.

Aurora Short (7)
St Peter-In-Thanet CE Junior School, St Peters

Basil The Bad

My name is Basil
The cat that is ginger
When night-time comes
I turn into a ninja.

I like rats
I like mice
I like things
I can terrorise.

I can open doors
I can play football
I eat cheese and lettuce
Because I'm so cool.

I'm such a slinky pussycat
I escape from my cat box
I really am a clever chap
More cunning than a fox.

Oliver Setterfield (10)
St Peter-In-Thanet CE Junior School, St Peters

What A Good Football Game

What a good game
We kick and scream
Start with a warm-up
That's the key to a successful team
We walk on the pitch
And fall in a ditch
A player gets hurt
His foot gets injured
Only ten players now
But the game finishes
With everyone laughing and cheering
No one knows what will happen in a while
But we are all full of smiles
What a good game.

Mercie Miller (9)
St Peter-In-Thanet CE Junior School, St Peters

Drive A Submarine Around The Shops

My plan of driving a submarine around the shops
didn't quite go to plan...
I bumped into the wall of the mall,
My submarine broke down,
I couldn't drive on the ground,
When I pressed the pedal, I stood still,
I finally moved but crashed in the beauty aisle,
I moved again but crashed in every food aisle,
And bumped into the shoppers
that were buzzing about.

Ethan Nicholas Cobley (9)
St Peter-In-Thanet CE Junior School, St Peters

My Pet Can Do Maths!

I have a fish that is clever and smart,
It can do maths in the beat of a heart.
Whether it's adding, multiplying, dividing or subtracting, my fish can do it all in a flash!
Although it has a three-second memory, it can add up numbers really quickly, quickly, quickly.
His friends in the tank think he's cool, you can train your brain and enjoy learning at fish school.

James Dowdeswell (10)
St Peter-In-Thanet CE Junior School, St Peters

Dreamland

Unicorns are magical mystical things
When their tails shake
All the birds start to sing
Fairy dust and rainbows appear in the sky
I can see them shimmering from where I lie
Snow-covered trees are starting to glisten
Children are laughing, listen
Fairies are magical mystical things
When their wings flutter
All the birds start to sing.

Evie Van Jensen (9)
St Peter-In-Thanet CE Junior School, St Peters

Sunbathing On A Cloud

I was comfy,
I was cosy,
And I was very dozy,
My head was at rest,
I knew I had done my best,
Now my work was through,
And everywhere was blue,
I knew I deserved this,
Then I felt like I was missing the cloud...
Oh no! I was just dreaming,
Then there was some grey smoke,
"What's that? Steam...?"

Bradley Tournay (10)
St Peter-In-Thanet CE Junior School, St Peters

Beautiful Cosy Cloud Snooze

I was comfy,
I was cosy,
And I was very, very dozy,
My head was at rest,
I felt like the best,
An alien helped me to speak,
A pigeon had a peek,
Now the day was done,
The alien had gone,
I would rest again at dawn,
On the lawn,
And have a dream,
That would be filled with steam.

Thomas Girdler (9)
St Peter-In-Thanet CE Junior School, St Peters

Pokémon

Come on, come on
I love Pokémon
Pikachu and Charmeleon
Are my favourite ones
I do like others from
Generation One

I like a couple from
Generation Two
Cyndaquil and Pichu
To name a few.

The journey
Still goes on
Pikachu
I choose you!

Harlan Groombridge (9)
St Peter-In-Thanet CE Junior School, St Peters

T-Rex's Rainbow Farting Problem!

What is that over there?
It is not a bear,
Is it a T-rex?
Wow, it really is!
But what is it doing?
It is not mooing,
It smells like candy,
Is it just sandy?
Oh no!
Here comes my crow,
He knows what it is,
He says,
"It is a T-rex farting rainbows!"

Niamh Lily Carroll (9)
St Peter-In-Thanet CE Junior School, St Peters

A Water Volcano

I've stood here for centuries being dormant
Nobody alive has ever known me to erupt
But now I feel something roaring up inside me
I've gathered a crowd to watch me blow
Magma and lava up so high? No!
Whoosh!
A jet of water
A big splash
Everyone is soaked.

Rex Beevers (9)
St Peter-In-Thanet CE Junior School, St Peters

Unicorn Land

I saw a unicorn today...
It was having a bath on top of a rainbow,
Lilac glittery water spilt over the edges,
Pink candyfloss clouds floated by,
Tiny fairies danced on top of the bubbles
To disco music,
Everyone was having such a good time,
I couldn't believe my eyes!

Sophia Poppy Davidge (8)
St Peter-In-Thanet CE Junior School, St Peters

The Best Footballer In The World

Ronaldo, Ronaldo, I'm coming after you,
You'd better watch out, just give it a year or two,
I'll be running down the wing,
Whilst the gaffer shouts a thing,
It's amazing what you can do,
But I'll become better than you,
And I'll even pay my taxes too.

Sam Gibson (9)
St Peter-In-Thanet CE Junior School, St Peters

Football Poem

F ancy people showing off their skills, kicking the ball with the back of their heels
O n my head
O ver the top
T o the striker, the
B all can be scored
A goal is scored!
L oved it
L ove it.

Mason Buckingham (10)
St Peter-In-Thanet CE Junior School, St Peters

In A Thunderstorm Twist

I felt the rain, wind and hail,
And then the thunder and lightning came,
The thunder banged and popped,
It was shocking and it roared loudly,
Destroying everything: trees, houses and logs,
I got scared but it was soon gone, yay!

Mia-Brooke Aimee Page (8)
St Peter-In-Thanet CE Junior School, St Peters

My Weird Family

I have a very, very weird family,
My mother is an alien and goes out in the night,
My father is a genie and his bangs
give me an awful fright!
My brother... my brother is the prime minister
and... yeah, let's just call it a night.

When the morning comes,
I see my little brother sipping coffee,
My dad is wishing for some banoffee,
My mother is still not back yet... obviously.

In the afternoon, we go for a walk,
As soon as I see the stares we're getting,
I know this is a bad idea
and we shouldn't have dared,
My mother takes us back into her spaceship, yay!
By the time we are in the house,
my dad wishes for a colossal bowl of ice cream,
My family may be weird,
but I love them very much.

Faida Aghogho Okotete (11)
Temple Mill Primary School, Strood

To Ride A Lightning Bolt

I often wonder how it would feel,
To sit upon a cloud and eat a meal,
To gaze upon rainbows after the rain,
Instead of looking at them
through the window pane,
Watching the clouds as they form together,
Taking a guess at what would happen
to the weather,
Jumping from clouds as they crashed with a jolt,
And stepping onboard a lightning bolt,
Darting through the sky with a whizz and a bang,
"Faster, let's go faster!" is what I would sing,
Zigging and zagging this way and that,
Trying to hold on with my hand on my hat,
All too soon it would come to an end,
As we'd approach the rainbow
and round the bend,
I'd slide down the slope
where it touched the ground
And step onto Earth all safe and sound.

I'd get back in the house - all normal it would seem
I'd look out of the window to continue my dream.

Rebecca Bragg (11)
Temple Mill Primary School, Strood

A Chest Grabbed My Mum

A chest gobble my mum,
it just snatched her by her very bum.
Before she realised, it was too late,
and she accepted her fate.

A shark drank my dad,
it was extremely sad.
He went through its throat,
then he saw a boat.

A cloud suffocated my nan,
I wasn't really a big fan.
She lived next to me,
as you now cannot see.

Now all of my family is gone,
this place is a real con!

Henry Williams (10)
Temple Mill Primary School, Strood

The Dog Monster

The unforgotten
The beast
The powerhouse

It is Dug
He is as cute as a pug
But as fierce as a tiger
He's an almighty fighter
His beautiful brown coat
Is worth a good boast
His floppy ears help him hear
And are only a small part of his gear

Big-eyed
Flat-nosed
Fat body

You can never mistake him, it's Dug!

Martin Poprelkov (11)
Temple Mill Primary School, Strood

The Swimming Competition

I went to school one day
And I heard people shouting hooray!
I asked why and why and why?
What was the answer I got?
"We're going to a swimming competition today!"
I thought I might cry,
I had been waiting for this for a long time.

I got changed as quick as I could
When we were finished, my teacher said,
"Put on your hoods."
So I put on my hood and ran into line
We went up the hill and the bus was there
The bus was quick
We were there in a flick!

When we were there, I jumped in the pool
Everyone stared at me, I wondered why
Then I realised...
I was a penguin!

I tried to swim to the end of the pool
And hide myself in the deep water,
But I went too fast,
I bashed my head on the wall,
I looked at my class, they all stared,
I felt so small...

Chloe Tippin (8)
The Granville School, Sevenoaks

When I Took A Penguin To Sea

When I woke one day, I jumped with glee
because I remembered I was going to the sea,
I ran down to the beach
with my bucket and spade,
Oh no!
I saw a penguin next to a hearing aid!
What?
I thought, *how can this be?*
I looked again but this time,
he was pecking happily at an ice cream,
I cautiously walked over and said hi,
And then he took my hand
and took me to the sand dunes,
He pushed the ice cream in my face
and shoved me in the sand,
An hour later, I was still covered in sand,
That was it, I had had enough,
I stomped away.

Harriet Mackenzie (8)
The Granville School, Sevenoaks

When I Took A Penguin To Space

I once went to space,
What I didn't notice was that there was
a penguin in my suitcase!
He ate all my sun cream,
Now that was a mess,
He vomited it out,
And all I found at first,
Was the stuff floating around,
Then out came the penguin,
All chubby and fat,
He was covered in sun cream
from his head to his toes,
I didn't know penguins could be so messy,
So when he was sleeping,
I chucked him out the window,
And he flew to Mars.

Lexie Beck (8)
The Granville School, Sevenoaks

The Day My Family Turned Into Penguins

When I woke up one morning,
I smelt something weird,
Was it the sea? Coral? Oh no!
It was worse than I'd feared!
Argh! My family were penguins!
My mum was eating her hair,
My brother was eating his toys,
And my dad was the worst,
He was eating everything in sight!

Madeleine Soong (7)
The Granville School, Sevenoaks

A Day Out With My Penguin

I didn't know quite what penguins liked to do,
So I went and bought one and went to the zoo,
And he ate my ponytail, then he weed in my shoe,
What naughty things penguins do!
I thought I should put him in a car
and then put it in the sea,
But then my cute, naughty penguin ran up a tree!
It was time to go home,
but my penguin was no more,
Maybe one day, he would row back to shore.

Isabel Mclain (7)
The Granville School, Sevenoaks

A Penguin Came To Tea

One afternoon, when my gran was sleeping,
a penguin came for tea!
He asked me if I'd hurt myself, I said, "My knee!"
But all he said was that he needed a pee!
So when it went to bed, I sneaked inside its bag,
A cookbook? What a funny thing to have!
So I looked inside the book
and I found a big surprise,
A recipe for silly snake spaghetti!

Jessica Dowell (7)
The Granville School, Sevenoaks

Class Three

I woke up in the morning, ready to go to school,
My first day of Year 3,
I hoped it would be cool but,
To my surprise, my teacher was a penguin!
First, she taught us how to catch fish.
What? I thought, *I can't catch fish!*
Next, she taught us how to waddle,
"Waddle!" she said. "Waddle, waddle, waddle!"

Amelie Cassidy (7)
The Granville School, Sevenoaks

A Trip To The Zoo

One day, I went to the zoo
I saw a penguin juggling goo!
The penguin gave me a look
As if he wanted me to cook:
a bowl of sand soup
a worm pie
a log sandwich
a hawk kebab
a crocodile hamburger
a coral salad
dog bolognese
some monkey sushi
and even snake noodles!

Alexandra Rose Sinclair (7)
The Granville School, Sevenoaks

Tickle Monster

When you're sad, he'll appear by you,
He's the tickle monster,
His job is to make you feel better,
So when you're sad, don't be afraid,
He'll appear by you to make you laugh,
He tickles you,
He's so much fun,
He's harmless, you see,
Be his friend cos he's so kind to anyone,
He'll let you choose the game,
You'd better be quick choosing the game
Or he'll disappear,
You see, he's such a friendly tickle monster,
He gives you no harm, you see,
So be the tickle monster's friend.

Maya Jheeta (7)
Upton Primary School, Bexley

Superhero School

Hooray, hooray,
today is my first day,
I'm so excited I could scream,
and joyfully beam.

Today, today,
was my first day,
I have made a very benevolent friend,
that will stick with me until the end.

Yay, yay,
today is my second day,
I will learn how to fight,
with all my might.

Today, today,
was my second day,
I cannot fight,
maybe in a few weeks, I might.

Hooray, hooray,
today is my fifteenth day,

over time, I have been practising my fighting skills,
it gives me such a thrill.

Today, today,
was my fifteenth day,
I have perfected my fighting,
it has paid off, trying and trying.

Yay, yay,
today is my thirtieth day,
I will finally get to use my superpower,
in front of my enemies, I will not cower.

Today, today,
was my thirtieth day,
I used my icy powers,
for hours and hours.

Hooray, hooray,
today is my fiftieth day,
I'm still practising,
no more I find it challenging.

Today, today,
was my fiftieth day,

I can now freeze my foes,
even if they aren't very close.

Yay, yay,
today is my fifty-fifth day,
I will arrest many bad guys,
without the help of any allies.

Today, today,
was my fifty-fifth day,
I imprisoned two baddies today,
hooray, hooray.

From today, I am now known as Ice Girl,
the newest superhero in the world!

Maya Fahim (10)
Upton Primary School, Bexley

The Dragon's Cave

The dragon is breathing water,
People are swimming in the grass,
Mushrooms are changing colour
When the dragon comes out of the cave,
People having fun,
People having a bath underneath the dragon,
People going wild,
Digging grass while swimming,
The dragon soaking everyone,
Mushrooms getting squashed,
Dragons going crazy,
Mushrooms shining in the dark,
Everyone going wild and funny!

Gunjan Uppal (8)
Upton Primary School, Bexley

The Brave Little Fox

At dawn,
The brave little fox returns,
The dead tree awaits,
In the deepest part of the mystical forest,
She gets the key,
Unlocks the door of the tree,
With a hollow space inside,
Making a perfect home,
And what she finds there is... a rose,
It is unusual,
More like a tulip but still a rose,
She picks it up,
And she stares at it,
The faint morning star is glowing,
Glowing far more than usual,
The rose starts shrivelling up,
The brave little fox knows it is the first day of autumn,
The door creaks,
And a gust of wind rushes past her,
Mr Fox is waiting there,

Surrounded by falling autumn leaves,
Mr Fox is waiting for breakfast,
What a wonderful day it has been.

Masha Strazdina (9)
Upton Primary School, Bexley

My Adventure In Wood Wonders!

What a strange place,
Wood Wonders is,
Magical keys,
That open doors in trees,
Books talking,
While I'm walking,
Reading their stories aloud,
Mysterious and magical,
Elegant and enchanting,
I ride over the hills on a lightning bolt,
Shrieking, "Halt!"
I see elves,
Climbing onto shelves,
Bouncing and pouncing,
Red jumbo-sized mushrooms dancing,
And ballerinas prancing,
Flowers keep growing as big as giants,
Through without being defiant,

Everything is so grand,
What a magical wonderland!

Arisha Rahman (9)
Upton Primary School, Bexley

Living The Dream Like Candy Queens!

Life is good like a piece of pud,
Rocking candy like we should,
Dogs have lots of strawberry hairs,
Our servants are made out of gummy bears,
We have a tree that's a chocolate log,
The leaves on it are hot dogs,
Light bulbs are made out of doughnuts,
We like to shout, "Nice to dough you!"
Our buses are made out of Double Deckers,
We're living the dream like candy queens!

Liana Wallace (8) & Esmee Jones (9)
Upton Primary School, Bexley

Young Writers Information

We hope you have enjoyed reading this book – and that you will continue to in the coming years.

If you're a young writer who enjoys reading and creative writing, or the parent of an enthusiastic poet or story writer, do visit our website **www.youngwriters.co.uk**. Here you will find free competitions, workshops and games, as well as recommended reads, a poetry glossary and our blog. There's lots to keep budding writers motivated to write!

If you would like to order further copies of this book, or any of our other titles, then please give us a call or visit **www.youngwriters.co.uk**.

Young Writers
Remus House
Coltsfoot Drive
Peterborough
PE2 9BF
(01733) 890066
info@youngwriters.co.uk

Join in the conversation!
Tips, news, giveaways and much more!

f YoungWritersUK   **🐦** @YoungWritersCW